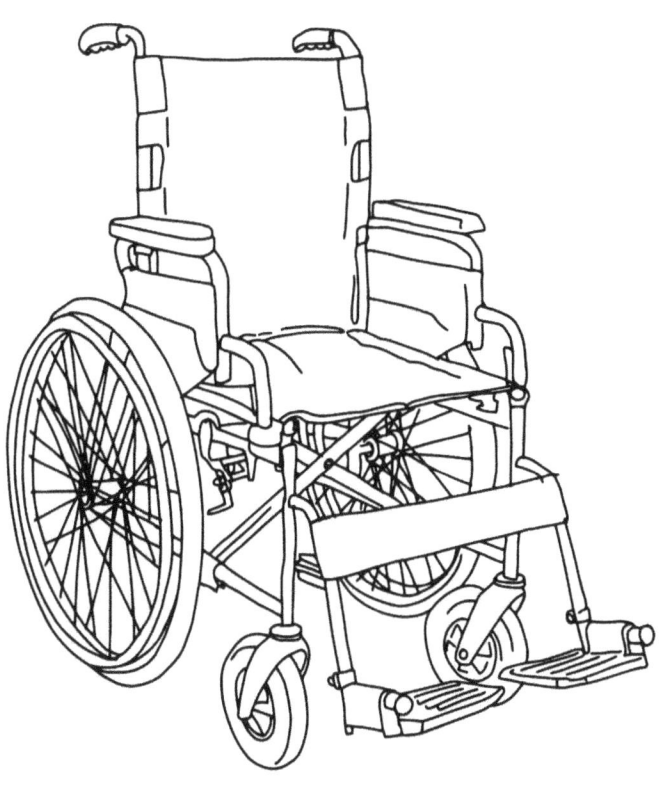

Copyright © 2021 Amie M Marie
Mandells House Publishing
www.amiemarie.co.uk

First edition: January 2022
Second edition: February 2023

ISBN 978-1-8383769-4-9 (paperback)
ISBN 978-1-8383769-5-6 (ebook)

Art by Serkan Özbay

Performance rights and actor scripts are available through Cyberpress's site: www.StagePlays.com, or by email admin@stageplays.com

Performance rights are required whether or not an audience pays admission. The only time this script may be performed without charge is in a private home, for audition, or in a classroom.

Thank you for always being there for me and inspiring me to follow my dreams, Karen Grace Goodwin.

Thank you for your kind words of encouragement, Pip Vigo and Ann McFarran.

For disabled people without families or charities in their corner.

"We have heard literally thousands of accounts of the stress and suffering caused by the assessment […] The human cost is immeasurable." - Frank Field, Labour MP (2017)

"It's shocking that so many of those trying to claim this benefit are in fact well enough to do some kind of work. Reform is needed so those who can work are helped to find a job and not left trapped on benefits. Sadly there are those who see being 'on the sick' as an easy option."– Emma Boon, TaxPayers' Alliance (2011)

"It may be carried out by an institution rather than an individual, but it's still abuse. It's almost faceless because it's being perpetrated by a department of government. But the impact on us is still the same." – Alice Kirby, interviewed by The Guardian (2017)

"We can't just leave people and say you've filled a form in, sent it off and that means you're on the benefit for life." – Mike Penning, Disability Minister, Conservative MP (2013)

"The purpose of PIP was never to address the needs of disabled people. It was to cruelly slash the help that so many depend upon to be able to take part in society." – Linda Burnip, Disabled People Against Cuts (2018)

"We have left people on welfare for year after year when [disabled] people, with help and with assistance, could work." – David Cameron, Prime Minister (2011)

Characters

> DINO
> ABBY THOMSON
> CAROL JOYCE
> HANNAH JOYCE
> EMPLOYER
> TELEVISION
> WOMAN
> MAN
> SPEAKER
> NADINE DORRIES
> JUNE PIERCE
> JOSH SANDHU

Act 1, Scene 1.

Two strangers, angled facing each other. DINO is a 55 year old man in a tatty suit. It is hard to tell if the suit was damaged only today from a stumble or has been worn down. ABBY is a 25-ish woman, with a glamorous ankle-length skirt, a smart blouse and an old, well-used backpack.

DINO: I study the universe.

ABBY: *(direct address)* I had the distinct feeling I was talking to a god.

DINO: I study the universe.

ABBY: *(direct address)* Not that I believe in gods, or subscribe to any religion.

At this point, through sound and flickering lighting, it becomes clear that the pair are on a train. Late evening. They are sat opposite each other. They sway on their seats.

DINO: I try to keep an eye on down here, you know, but I can't do anything about it. Up there *(he points to the ceiling),* that's what I'm about.

ABBY: *(direct address)* Plato's Prime Mover is what I thought of. It's what occurred to me, um, the theory that if there is a god they, well, caused everything by moving the first thing, but now have nothing to do with us.

DINO: I've got a feeling, it's soon. Whoosh.

ABBY: *(direct address)* Anyway, uh. 9.14pm, the Stansted express line carrying me home, out of London. I was just travelling through, keeping myself to myself.

DINO: There's three ways it can go. Categorized in two: natural disasters; earthquakes and that. Manmade, nuclear: boom. Crazy, crazy. Got that Jim - in Korea, Putin nearer-by, an' America. *(pointing to the ceiling)* But they forget, they don't think.

> Out there, like before, the dinosaurs. Happened before, it'll happen again.

ABBY: *(direct address)* Something about this man held my, *(searching for the word)* gaze, and I had the distinct feeling I was talking to a. Something far more intelligent than, than anyone can simply appear. An equal, of mine, but from a different plane of existence? Something about him was settled, still as ice melting in a jar, or like calm water, a reflection – my reflection – in a black, inky pond, behind the buzz of warm cheeks, flickering eyebrows, and shoulders that swayed with the train tracks beneath us. It was like meeting *me* but *male* and *fifty*. And. He was drunk.

DINO: They think I'm mad. You think I'm mad.

ABBY: No.

DINO: I'm not mad. I'm intelligent, I *think* about things. *(he tilts his head)* You're the same.

	But you're not confident. *(a beat)* I could change the world. You could, too.
ABBY:	*(direct address)* I had work in the morning. Or at least, an interview for work – in the morning.
DINO:	They think we're mad. *(a beat)* That, *(he clicks his fingers)* evolution guy.
ABBY:	Darwin.
DINO:	Ah, you know. Him. He was onto something. I read his – I, he was nearly right.
ABBY:	*(direct address)* I said nothing.
DINO:	The sun's gonna go. One million. That's what I bet, one million, whoosh. Later, white dwarf, last a billion years. Earth's 4.5 million, white dwarf? Billion.
ABBY:	So at five and a half million-?

DINO: Yes! Sun goes, whoosh. White dwarf, we go to Mars.

ABBY: But that's further away, but I guess white dwarfs *are* hotter?

DINO: *(nods.)* S'coming. They're not telling us.

ABBY: I doubt they would.

DINO: You look very nice, elegant. Old style but modern. / What station is it?

ABBY: Thanks.

DINO: I can't see well.

ABBY: We're at Harlow Town. Harlow Mill is next.

DINO: Thanks. What's your name?

ABBY: Abby. Nice to meet you.

DINO: Dino. Stay safe.

ABBY: I plan to.

DINO: Tell me about you.

ABBY: What is there to say?

DINO: Something. Always. There's always something, that's the joy.

ABBY: Um, I'm unemployed, but not for long. I – I like cats, but really I like turtles? I like the way they / swim.

DINO: What do you fear?

ABBY: Big question! Death, I suppose?

DINO: *(laughs)* No you don't.

ABBY: *(laughs)* No, I don't.

DINO: You don't like men.

ABBY is silent.

DINO: You're scared. Of me, of men.

There is a long pause.

ABBY: They're... threatening, sometimes, I suppose.

DINO: Hmm.

ABBY: I had... my ex wasn't nice. He put me in *so much* debt. I'm still paying for -

Another pause. The train slows.

DINO: I got a wife, kids. Don't see them anymore. But they're pretty, love, so *warm*. Makes you feel warm just to, just t'glance. Look.

DINO pulls out his wallet and shows off a stamp-sized picture.

DINO: This is b'fore she changed her hair. His tooth's grown back in, too. Taller, him. He likes the ocean. Big mysteries, big minds, real knowledge're after. His man's the sky and beyond, me boy the underlands. And her – she's my Persephone. Both, all, everything. Life.

ABBY: Yeah.

DINO: Tell me about you.

ABBY: I'm lonely. Plants and cat videos can only do so much.

DINO: And the stars?

ABBY: They're distant. And flicker.

DINO: But they're there.

ABBY: I can't see them in the day. And I'm inside at night.

DINO: Then you're the one ignoring them.

The train comes to a stop. DINO must leave.

DINO: Let's have a kiss goodbye.

ABBY: No thank you!

DINO: On the hand?

ABBY: *(with a laugh)* Why not?

DINO bows and holds ABBY's hand lightly, bringing it to his lips. They share a moment. The train beeps for the doors to shut. DINO leaps out.

ABBY: *(calling out)* I'm pleased I met you!

Lights fade.

ABBY: *(direct address)* Strange man.

Act 1, Scene 2.

A ticking clock. Light shift to reveal a cramped living room, slightly cluttered, with a small table beside the upstage window. This is the only detailed set; more real, recognizable, and comforting than anywhere else. CAROL lives here. She is approachable – unintimidating – and unremarkable, save some odd scabs and bruises along her exposed arms. She has a small plaster on her cheek, and one foot is in a support brace. Spare crutches are leaned nearby, and a front door exists upstage. She wears warm colours.

CAROL hums, jolly, pausing to take large breaths between musical phrases and to lean on her crutch. She carefully picks up items from a box that's been stacked to her waist height, and we see that it contains fragile, speckled glass ornaments. With considered slowness, CAROL turns to the dull tree in the corner of the room and hangs the ornaments. CAROL can only raise her arms to shoulder height and so the top third of the tree goes bare.

At the window comes a clumsy cat who paws at the glass. CAROL pauses, looks for the source of the sound then goes to open the window. She tuts to encourage the cat closer.

CAROL: What's your name, darling? Have you got – where's your collar, little one? Hm?

The cat backs away. CAROL peels the ham from a sandwich and offers it to the cat.

CAROL: Well, you must be new. I don't know *you*, mister. You're not Smokey and you're not Oscar. God knows who else owns a cat around here.

The cat is not enticed.

CAROL returns to decorating at her own speed. She hums, quieter, and stops abruptly when an ornament falls from the tree and smashes. CAROL jolts and sighs. The cat nabs the ham and scarpers out the window, inadvertently pushing the sandwich and plate from the table to the floor.

CAROL must rest for a time and settles on a chair with a comfortable blanket. It is peaceful. A clock ticks.

Envelopes are forced through the letter box and land with a weighty thud.

CAROL jerks, fearful. She sees the post. The fear does not leave her.

Slowly, grimacing with some break-through pain, she leans forwards and starts to rock herself slightly. She uses her arms to push herself from the chair in time with a large swing forwards. CAROL stumbles, braces to fall, but doesn't. After a beat, CAROL turns in little steps to face her crutch. She uses it to move from the living room to the front door.

CAROL then pauses, readjusts her weight, and uses the base of the crutch to push at the envelopes, sussing out what has arrived today. At a brown, A4 envelope she panics.

She sits back down. Stares at the door. At the wall. Ticking of a clock. Scratches her hands until she bleeds; gnaws her lips, picks her scalp. The light changes from morn to noon to night. With the exception of such self-harm, CAROL has been static with anxiety. The Christmas tree continues to flash red in the half-light. The ticking clock speeds up.

Act 1, Scene 3.

The clock stops. HANNAH enters, clinking her door keys as she puts them away. She turns on the lights, until the stage is a cosy colour. HANNAH, mid-twenties, is both upbeat and bone-tired. She wears a retail uniform.

HANNAH: *(calling out)* Hey mum, I got milk. They were out of red so I got green.

CAROL hastens to meet her. Grimacing at a wrong move. At some point the TV is accidentally turned on; it plays static in the background.

CAROL: *(hiding her pain)* How was it?

HANNAH: They were out of red so I got green.

CAROL: And your day?

HANNAH: Fine; they were out of red milk.

CAROL: Train was late.

HANNAH: How's you? Oh, and the eggs are off. I guess I'll pick some up tomorrow then.

CAROL: Was / Kenny-?

HANNAH: Kenny was a twat today, though. Fucking can't wait for his transfer. Had a funny customer today though, kinda like the Purple Hat Incident but not nearly as good. Mum?

Silence.

HANNAH: Mum?

CAROL: Got some post.

HANNAH: Oh, ok. Good? Anything you were expecting?

CAROL: It's the. *(a pause)* Got some post. The usual.

HANNAH: Oh? Anything you were expecting?

CAROL: Nothing unusual.

HANNAH: Ok. *(a beat)* Is pasta alright by you tonight?

CAROL: Not tonight.

HANNAH: IBS?

CAROL: Was on the toilet for hours this morning. I don't think I can eat tonight. You should though. I've not been able to keep anything down, either. Nothing unusual.

HANNAH: Have you eaten today? Not even the sandwich I left out?

CAROL: I tried. I, a ca-, I dropped it.

HANNAH: I'll make you a cuppa at least. *(a pause)* Where'd you drop it? The sandwich. I'll pick it up before it ruins the carpet. Oh, no worries, I see it through here. You sit down.

HANNAH shoos CAROL to her chair, then bins the fallen sandwich.

HANNAH: Hang on, is that – is the tree up?

CAROL: Yes, I thought I'd –

HANNAH: You're feeling ok? You didn't strain yourself did you?

CAROL: Only a little.

HANNAH: I could've done it for you.

CAROL: I wanted to do something for myself, for once.

HANNAH: I just don't want you to be in pain. I could've done it for you.

CAROL: Hannah, I'm always in pain. But I wanted to do something nice – for us.

HANNAH: Mum, it's November.

CAROL: It's not *too* soon.

HANNAH: It's November the *first*.

CAROL: The shops will be playing Christmas music.

HANNAH: That's not a *real* measurement of time.

CAROL: It's almost nearly Christmas season, and we're going to have a good one.

HANNAH: *(a beat)* Of course. *(They hug)* Love you, mum.

CAROL: I love you loads, too.

HANNAH: Love you mo - /

CAROL: Most! Hah! I win.

HANNAH: For the first and last time, mum. How was your day?

CAROL: Same old, Hannah. Nothing unusual. Got some post. Didn't eat, IBS. Must've slept funny, my back ached so I switched to the chair. Tried reading but couldn't get past the first page, my eyes blurred, I kept rereading and reading and reading. It's frustrating. I used to have a wonderful imagination.

HANNAH: I remember.

CAROL: I'd come up with whole movie scripts in my head before bed, then regret never writing them down.

HANNAH: I remember.

CAROL: They had such twists, such turns! They should've been made. They'd be such successes.

HANNAH: And you'd cast /

CAROL: I'd cast them, based on the celebrities of the day. Who I'd want as who, and often I'd put my friends like Marina or Paula in the big roles because I knew they'd've liked that.

HANNAH: I remember. Is Paula the one in London or Berlin? With the son who -

CAROL: I'm not sure where she is now. But I met her in London, we went to school together. We were best friends until Louise took me

>   to Italy instead of her. But she came to my
>   wedding. Her son died last year.

HANNAH: *Do* we know anyone in Berlin?

CAROL: I don't think so, Hannah.

HANNAH: Oh. I was so sure. So, gold and red for the tree this year?

CAROL: They're my favourite colours.

HANNAH: Oh, you've switched back to red?

CAROL: I was blue for so long, but red has always been my colour.

HANNAH: So you switched back to red. Ah, is any of this for me?

HANNAH picks up the post.

HANNAH: Is this -? It looks official. Is it something about money?

CAROL: It came in a brown envelope. I thought it'd be white, that's what the group said.

HANNAH: It looks official.

CAROL: I can't open it. I can't. I've tried all day to – but I'm. What if this is the time they say that I'm not -

HANNAH: It's official. Don't stress. Let's not. Just, remember. You aren't faking. You're real, just be honest and they'll see that. Officially.

CAROL: I know it's –

HANNAH: It's just to stop others cheating the system.

CAROL: I know. Preventing fraud. Proving things. I'm just worried.

HANNAH: Worried?

HANNAH throws the envelopes down onto a side table in frustration. She tuts.

HANNAH: Scaremongers is what they are. Those stories you hear, not real. They're upset at getting caught. Look, I'll help you fill it out after dinner. It won't be that difficult. After all it's for any kind of disability, right? Even those who struggle mentally – so it's gotta be easy to pass. *That's* how the cheaters get through, mum, it's vague and easy because the bloody government is incompetent and wants to help everyone, even the people who don't deserve it. It's all the news ever talks about, and ordinary folk have to be vigilant and report fraudsters, like, do it themselves because the council won't do their jobs right.

CAROL: I know. I know that. I'm just worried. Preventing fraud. I'm just worried.

HANNAH: Pretty sure Rachel reported this guy a few weeks back, saw him walking to his car. *(HANNAH jolts)* Hang on, it's B.

CAROL: B?

HANNAH: From school, she did uni. She's back in town tomorrow. *(HANNAH answers her*

>   *phone)* Hi B! How's it going? ... Ok... Nah,
>   I'm at home, you? Oh, need a lift? Ok,
>   why's that? ...Ahh. Yeah. Oooh, good luck.
>   Of course I'm wishing you luck, hun.
>   BBF's, yeah? You'd wish *me* happiness.
>   Get gotta have a get together -

HANNAH exits. We hear a gas hob be lit and pasta boils as HANNAH presumably continues her conversation off stage.

CAROL opens the first page of the form. She reads carefully.

CAROL: Got to face the fear, work through it. It's open now. I can't put it off. Pen. I'm just worried. Pen, pen, pen.

CAROL searches, slowly, leaning on her stick. She is otherwise mobile. She finds one, but her grip is poor and it falls to the ground. She pauses but does not attempt to retrieve it. She searches for another pen, but does not find one.

CAROL: *(Calling for help)* Hannah.

There is no reply. CAROL leans against a wall and tries to use her stick to roll the pen into a different position, closer. Without the stick beside her, CAROL overbalances and nearly falls. CAROL tries again, leaning on the stick and using a foot to adjust the pen. CAROL makes a pained sound but keeps trying. CAROL then tries to use the pen as a support to crouch lower to the ground. She grabs the pen but falls entirely. She is in some pain. She readjusts into a sitting position, leaning on the same door frame as before. Both pen and stick are far from her. She breathes through the pain. CAROL slowly pulls herself into all fours and crawls to her walking stick and grabs the pen while she's there. She then must crawl to a chair. She puts her items down at the base of the chair. She puts her hands on the seat of the chair and pulls her torso onto the seat. She takes a break. She then puts her hands on the arms of the chair and at once pulls her torso higher and swivels to throw her bum onto the seat. She is exhausted. She then must get up to fetch a reaching-stick from the side table. She takes a long time and uses the wall to support her.

She then returns to the chair, use the grab stick with difficulty to raise the items from the ground. The pen is tricky. Once both are retrieved, CAROL leaves the reaching-stick on the chair, unable to face walking to put it back. Pen and stick in hand, CAROL returns to the form. She is pale, in pain, and tired; or at least, more so than before. She resumes.

CAROL: Tell us about: tablets or medication, any treatments you're having such as *(beat)* any side effects these – ok. I can. I need my, my prescription list to check. That's upstairs. *(Calling for her)* Hannah.

HANNAH: *(off stage)* Yeah?

CAROL: *(Calling)* Can you come here?

A long silence.

HANNAH: *(off stage)* Mum, did you want something?

Silence. HANNAH enters.

HANNAH: Did you call me? I thought I just heard you.

CAROL: Yes, I did, I, can you get my prescription for the, it's for the form. Can you-?

HANNAH: Yeah, of course. Let me stir the pasta once then I'll run up. Oh, hey, yeah – when's that Pain Management course of yours starting? I need to book shifts around –

CAROL: December.

HANNAH hums in thought, exits and returns after a time. CAROL is now holding her side, body tense, as a reoccurring pain throbs. HANNAH passes the paper.

HANNAH: How goes it? Are you ok?

CAROL: Yes, it's just. *(She pauses)* I'm at the start.

HANNAH: How long is it? Twenty pages, most? Need to take a break?

CAROL: No, no. I've barely done anything yet.

HANNAH: Ok.

CAROL starts to copy words and phrases from her prescription list. She struggles.

HANNAH: They're struggling to find a replacement for Katie at work. Meant it was crazy busy, but that's ok because it just improves my stats I suppose. Bigger bonus, because I processed more but haven't done longer shifts. But they're asking people to take on more hours. And of course I've said no, because, though, like we could use the money, but they're gonna ask again if they don't find a, or they might anyway. They'll call it a promotion, probably, but it's not one technically. So I might bite the bullet and take on a few more hours in my contract, share the load, get paid more per hour if it's that way rather than just doing them as extra shifts, you know, but only if Hazel lets me be super flexible, I thought. Just in case you had a bad day or a few in a row, or hospital things. Some of them might be at a different branch, too, which means I might be further away some

	days but it would mean we could save up for the bathroom conversion quicker.
CAROL:	I, I don't want you to turn things down though. You could go for it. Career progression is important.
HANNAH:	I know. But it's ok.

HANNAH fetches two small bowls of pasta and cutlery. One set of cutlery is brightly coloured and bent; adapted.

HANNAH:	I can't leave you to just, struggle. Who'd buy the milk or fetch things or pick things up if you didn't call on me? Plus, if I earn much more then I don't know what that'll do to the council tax, and it's not like I'm a career girl, you know, mum. I never can be. I have you. Unless we got a trained dog or something, but how'd we even get one of those? And can it clean up its own poop? Now that's a question.
CAROL:	I didn't want any.

HANNAH: I know. But it's ok. It's no bother. Just in case you can manage a few bites.

CAROL: Maybe. *(A pause)* Hannah dear, do you mind writing them out for me. I can't, I can't read them it's –

HANNAH: Of course. It's ok. I know. Focus on eating.

CAROL: It's this, it's – brain fog. Can't see or feel or even understand through it. The world's a haze, distant, and the pain moist – condensation – damp and deep under the skin.

HANNAH: It's ok, mum. Don't worry. I don't mind. Where did you get to?

CAROL: Lyrica, Pregabalin.

HANNAH: Pregabalin, 300mg/day.

CAROLs eyes hurt and she is in more pain

HANNAH: If you want, we can *not* do it tonight? We can take tonight off.

CAROL waves that option away, rubbing at her forehead. HANNAH goes back to writing dutifully.

CAROL: *(direct address)* I hate this. I hate having to write about it, having to admit. It's depressing. I don't want to focus on what I can't do. I can't think. You don't know. It's not ok. Funny how I can think what this not, not, not-thinking is but not to think. I want to just live and do my best and *recover*. Try to, at least. Improving my health. It's like.

HANNAH: Shit.

CAROL: *(direct address)* that I'm faking. But that's what they make you think. It's not ok.

HANNAH: I didn't make you a tea.

CAROL: I don't /

HANNAH: No, no, I said I would so. Tea?

HANNAH leaves the room

CAROL: *(direct address)* My doctors say I am, that I am ill, and I have a blue badge, and my car got adapted, so I am. But am I? And I enough? Am I a good enough - ? When you think too hard about it, it /

HANNAH: *(off stage)* Decaf?

CAROL: *(direct address)* Am I not able to pick things up from the ground or am I just /

HANNAH: *(off stage)* I'm just going to assume, mum!

CAROL: *(direct address)* It's not that I don't want to be able to. But could I push through it more? I could force myself - it's not *impossible*, so saying "I can't" is a lie and we're all liars? I'd take more time than others, it'd hurt, but that doesn't make me disabled enough, does it?

The kettle boils.

CAROL: *(direct address)* I have two degrees. I had a business. A family. Everything they measure you by, as important and successful and goddamn human. This shouldn't be so bloody difficult.

Act 1, Scene 4.

An office meeting room. A job interview: a suited EMPLOYER jots on paperwork across from a nervous ABBY. Bright, artificial-feeling lights and stiff chairs. A ticking clock.

EMPLOYER: And you can start -?

ABBY: On Wednesday, but not before. If I get the job.

EMPLOYER: We'll be busy on Wednesday.

ABBY: Oh.

EMPLOYER: Tuesday works best.

ABBY: Oh, um.

EMPLOYER: *(dismissive)* We'll be in touch.

ABBY: *(quickly)* I can make Tuesday, to start, if that's necessary for the – if that's the only thing to ensure/

EMPLOYER: We'll be in touch. Do you have any questions?

ABBY: Not especially, no.

EMPLOYER: Then we'll be in touch. It was nice to meet each other, yes?

ABBY: Yes, um. You know, I. I feel like I should say why I wanted to interview, to try for this role though it, it is outside of my past experiences. And to-to reiterate that I have got the relevant work experience, and that I'm a quick worker and a quick learner, and you do good work, right? You help people. They come to you because they need to talk about their work, their life, their welfare. You help them. That's what any worker wants to believe they're doing.

EMPLOYER: Yes.

ABBY: Helping folk financially.

EMPLOYER: Yes.

ABBY: The people who qualify, who deserve it.

EMPLOYER: Yes.

ABBY: I'm a good worker. I'll turn up on time and I can stay late, and I don't mind if the air conditioning rattles and the windows are sealed shut. I-I've worked in all sorts of offices, I have the experience, the location, here, it suits me. I need a job, the rent - I had a thing on Tuesday but I can rearrange that if that's, if that's the difference. I just, I have bills to pay. We all do.

EMPLOYER: Yes. There's always a price.

ABBY: So I'll hear from you.

ABBY rises to leave.

ABBY: *(scolding herself)* Well done.

EMPLOYER: The probation period would last six weeks. At which point the pay grade will increase to reflect your status as a full member of

	the team. Then there will be a matter of commission, paid in addition to your hourly /
ABBY:	There's commission?
EMPLOYER:	Of course. Without commission how else would the staff follow our quotas?
ABBY:	Right.
EMPLOYER:	I warn you, your probationary period may continue past six weeks if you have not yet hit quota.
ABBY:	I see.
EMPLOYER:	Then we'll see you Tuesday.
ABBY:	Are you serious? Yes, thank you. Um, I'll see you – I'll be here. 9am?
EMPLOYER:	Six.
ABBY:	6am, yes, I-I I-can do that.

Act 1, Scene 5.

A return to the barren room; as before, two chairs and bright lights.

EMPLOYER: Are you ready?

ABBY nods. The EMPLOYER begins to fake a limp and walks towards ABBY. The EMPLOYER becomes a caricature of a disabled-scrounger.

EMPLOYER: *(with a put upon, rough voice)* Hello.

ABBY: Hello, my name is Abby Thom-/

EMPLOYER: *(as normal)* No! Do not give them your name.

ABBY: Why not?

EMPLOYER: It's a distraction. Only tell them if they ask, really insist. If they won't proceed without it. We don't want them looking you up after the assessment, friending you on Facebook. And you may be running late, so you wouldn't have the time for it.

ABBY: It would only take a second - /

EMPLOYER: And sixty seconds is a minute, and any more minutes of intentionally wasted time is time theft from this company and could lead to your unemployment.

ABBY: *(pause)* Noted.

EMPLOYER: *(again with the voice)* Hello.

ABBY: Hello. Your name is?

EMPLOYER: Smith.

ABBY: Smith. How are you today?

EMPLOYER: Good. *(with the voice)* Traffic was light, weather typical, and I am in no additional discomfort.

ABBY: Good. *(a beat)* You've come alone? I take it you drove here yourself?

EMPLOYER: The bus.

ABBY: Ah. I'll just get you a seat, hold on.

EMPLOYER: *(normal)* Let the claimant seat themselves.

There is a pause as EMPLOYER waits for ABBY to resume the roleplay.

ABBY: There's a seat over here for you.

ABBY points to the chair. EMPLOYER limps across the stage, and drags a chair a considerable distance before sitting down.

ABBY: And what is your diagnosis?

EMPLOYER: My leg, it isn't as it once was. There was accident at work.

ABBY: When was this accident?

EMPLOYER: A year ago.

ABBY: I take it you had physiotherapy?

EMPLOYER: I did.

ABBY: And did it help? Have you been offered more?

EMPLOYER: It didn't help. Nothing helps. *(EMPLOYER switches to their normal voice)* What have you noticed so far?

ABBY: Um, they-you, they have a limp in their left side after an accident at work. That claim will probably have come with supporting documents from their employer and GP, too - /

EMPLOYER: Disregard what they've sent in. You're observing what they do in the room. Now what else?

ABBY: Um, they walked across the room just fine – a bit slow but without visible pain /

EMPLOYER: Without pain, yes.

ABBY: And they also dragged that chair over, so they can carry at least – how much does that chair weigh?

EMPLOYER: Good so far, but you've missed some tricks. There's more you might've learnt in

	that same time. First, when the client walks in, you would normally-?
ABBY:	Oh, offer to shake their hand!
EMPLOYER:	Yes. Which lets you check for -/
ABBY:	Strength of grip, coordination, social awareness.
EMPLOYER:	What else?
ABBY:	Posture?
EMPLOYER:	and...?
ABBY:	Uh, ability to *(beat)* walk.
EMPLOYER:	Yes. Do they need the support they're claiming? You'd be surprised how many cycle to the assessment centre then *claim* they're bed-bound. Make sure you note down what they do at this point for the report, and enquire nicely *how* they travelled to the assessment. Be pleasant, tell them you only want to help, and they'll

	state the truth. Now, one of the first questions you are to ask is - /
ABBY:	Something about *(realising)* do they cook?
EMPLOYER:	Can they plan, prepare, and safely cook a three course meal?
ABBY:	Right. And the criteria says "can they do this reliably and without pain" so in their answer I should look for -
EMPLOYER:	That's what it *says*. But if they were in pain, they simply wouldn't do it. So if they say that they can, take that first answer. If they say that they can't, ask again.
ABBY:	OK.
EMPLOYER:	Abby, if they genuinely couldn't then they'd have starved to death and wouldn't be sat in the same room as you, getting assessed for benefits.

Silence.

EMPLOYER: You'll pick it up. Hardest thing is meeting the target.

ABBY: Oh, for commission.

EMPLOYER: Yes, but it's also a staff performance factor. We have to hit target. But you'll figure that out. Now, the physical aspects to the exam. It's easy enough, Abby. Ask them to stand, watch them stand. Ask them to walk, watch them walk. But you don't have to do this *every* assessment.. Don't be afraid to assume, and don't *feel bad* about sending back short reports, or copying and pasting between similar case files.

ABBY: Did you feel bad?

EMPLOYER: At first. But I think of it this way; if they *were* in need of P.I.P. then they'll definitely put in a Mandatory Reconsideration request or even take it to tribunal. A different department deals with those. It doesn't affect *our* statistics, so it won't reflect on us.

Act 1, Scene 6.

Static of a television, then a change of channel. We hear the following.

TV: According to disability charity Scope, it is more expensive to be disabled than to be able-bodied: on average it's an extra £570 every month, or £130 a week, as a result of managing their impairment and overcoming institutional barriers. P.I.P, the main benefit for the disabled in the UK, is worth just sixty pounds to ninety pounds each week and can be used to qualify for a rented disability-friendly vehicle. So has it gone wrong? Brought in to replace the Disability Living Allowance in 2013, Personal Independence Payments pays claimants in accordance with their genuine need. Claimants no longer show proof of disability diagnosis, but instead describe how that diagnosis disables them: does a

>   disability disable them? Does it stop
>   anyone from cleaning the dishes in their
>   home, or walking without pain? Is anyone
>   really disabled? Or are they lying? Now,
>   the weather.

Two chairs in a café. Distorted, ambient sounds. ABBY and HANNAH stir sugar sachets into their drink, but do not drink.

ABBY: How's your mum doing?

HANNAH: Usual.

ABBY: Hmm.

HANNAH: How's the flat?

ABBY: As you'd expect.

HANNAH: Hmm?

ABBY: Sorry, I don't mean to be vague.

HANNAH: I think I was, probably, too. Um, my mum's *(pause)* same old.

ABBY: Aw, no.

HANNAH: You?

ABBY: A bit crap.

HANNAH: She's going a bit downhill if I'm honest, but it's probably just a small relapse. She's not sleeping, but that's just the medication. Nothing we could do about it.

ABBY: My worries are a little small, compared.

HANNAH: Never. B, don't put yourself down just cos others are struggling. Besides, she's got me and I'm plenty. I shouldn't be complaining about it really. She's done so much for me over the years. I'm just paying it back.

ABBY: Makes me feel a little guilty I'm not as close to my mum.

HANNAH: Yeah, but you got to move out, in with Joe and all that.

ABBY: Ugh.

HANNAH: Sorry.

ABBY: No, no. I should be over it by now.

HANNAH: Well he didn't just *(she pauses, redirects)* Cheating is one thing, but saddling you with them debts and credit cards and loan sharks ain't on, B.

ABBY: I know that.

HANNAH: I'm here for you.

ABBY: I know that.

HANNAH: He was a crook.

ABBY: And I can't void those loans – we talked about this. Legally I *(a beat)* I don't want to get all worked up over it again, today. We've talked this to death, Hannah.

HANNAH: Yeah, sorry.

ABBY: Sorry, I shouldn't've snapped. And – and anyway, this job pays well, like, *really well.*

HANNAH: I got it.

ABBY: No, really well. Hannah, it starts at £36,000 a year *plus* commission. I'll be actually able to get out of debt and survive in the meantime.

HANNAH: That's / great.

ABBY: Then I'll be able to look into part ownership of the flat, maybe get a pet. Hannah, this could be so good for me. We could go out more, too – I'll spot you the cash. Bars, clubs, cafes! We always wanted to go abroad, maybe I could wrangle the gang together and /

HANNAH: Can I tell you something? I... I'm worried. More worried than even that time in year eight, B... I'm really worried about her. I think my mum's hiding something – from

> *me!* I can't think what it'd be but she's worried about something: she's blanking out at weird moments, and going silent in ways where she's, like, not losing her words from drowsiness or pain. It's not normal, not like her. It's not the meds... I think she might've been diagnosed with something awful, terminal and not - she doesn't want to tell me.

ABBY: Hannah.

HANNAH: I don't know what to do.

ABBY: She'll tell you, in her own time, Hannah. You just gotta, ride it out until then. *(beat)* Haven't I always been here for you? *(beat)* Come on, let's have a hug.

They do not move.

ABBY: Don't you feel better now?

HANNAH: I just feel like you're so far away, B. Like mum's all closed off, shrivelling up like a dead leaf – and you're a, a shadow of a bird passing me by, B.

ABBY: Don't you feel better?

HANNAH: I'm so alone.

ABBY: Don't you feel-?

Act 1, Scene 7.

A poorly lit sofa and TV. Static is shown to play and the television can be heard. ABBY sits, a mug in hand. She stares at the audience, blankly. HANNAH, headphones on and otherwise occupied with a book or phone. CAROL bites her nails until she bleeds. They are separate and alone.

TV: It's sheer laziness, and we can't keep rewarding laziness with financial security. Even chemo shouldn't stop folk from a shelf stacking role at their local; why else would they be getting treatment if not to work? Of course, the goal is to get sick and so-called-disabled people back into employment. Why else would they be loitering in our country, greedily sapping at the taxpayer's teet? See, the problem with the previous government is that people were being damned, condemned really. Before we created PIP, they were told that they were *so disabled* that they would get paid to never work, kept alive for no economic benefit, and thus never be reassessed. It's no surprise that we sought to change this. After all, it is the case that some degenerative conditions do get better. A percentage of people recover from terminal conditions, and the rest cease to claim any form of welfare.

We see DINO in dim, half-light.

DINO: You sleep and have forgotten me; you loved me living, but now that I am dead you think of me no further.

The TV goes dark. Light gets brighter on DINO.

TV: Did you know 80 people die *each* month after being declared "fit for work". And that's just the ones we know about.

Act 1, Scene 8.

A long silence. The distant sound of trains, coming and going. DINO sits alone.

DINO: The veil – between us and them. Us and the next. The next who were before and after, forever ago but *ain't* forever forwards, yeah? There comes an end. But what if I told you it weren't always separate. It's like – those ain't-sent... ancient jaguars right. Wi'd teeth. *(DINO gestures two sabre teeth with his hands)* We found one with Arthur in it's hip, made it all stiff and cranky. It should've died – but it didn't. Others made a community, helped it, kept it fed so that getting that arthritis didn't end the fella. *(Beat)* But the veil. That's where this started. And the veil *does* have a start. See, *(DINO rubs his face and pushes his hands through his hair.)* Giants, monsters, witches, wolves.

They weren't *(silence) over there*. They were with us, yeah? Then some, some – Vicky boy toff with a pipe says "they were over *there*" and the veil was - it was a line in the sand. Enlightenment. And those who get arth-arthur-teas *(beat)* can sod off. Survival o'fittest, yeah? Won't stop them. *(he points to the sky) Wooosh*. Stars are comin'.

Act 2, Scene 1.

A high-street with post-box centre stage. CAROL walks slowly with her stick. She is otherwise passing as able-bodied. Others walk by at speed, commenting as they approach or pass her, and leave the stage.

WOMAN: Hate slow walkers. Taking their time, like we've got all day.

The WOMAN aggressively knocks her shoulder into CAROL's, and hisses.

MAN: I'm sick of them using the disabled parking, then walking like nothing's the matter. Fuckers with fake badges. Where's the chair?

WOMAN: Ignore the chair. They can fake that too. I saw one get out of a chair once!

The MAN kicks CAROL's stick; she stumbles.

MAN: Disgusting.

WOMAN: Her eyebrows were drawn on, right? Ugly as fuckin' sin. Then she says she can't raise her arm, hold a pen. How'd they get on then? Did they grow that way? Skiving fuck.

CAROL: *(weakly)* They're natural.

WOMAN: You know what's not natural? Like, arms that don't grow, organs that don't function or "lose" function. You know? Them who act weird or look it. They're, like, defective. Defective people.

MAN: Don't belong.

WOMAN: Not right.

CAROL: It's the way things are.

CAROL arrives at the post-box. She pushes an envelope through the slot. DINO speaks to her, but she does not see him.

DINO: There can be no covenants between men and lions, wolves and lambs can never be

>   of one mind, but hate each other. See? We
>   lamb-limbed have no hope. There's no
>   understanding between us and them.

A woman who looks remarkably like the Conservative MP, NADINE DORRIES, stands from a height and speaks. CAROL passes by, ignored.

NADINE: If you know someone on benefits and they tweet, report them. They're con-artists, the lot. If they can use a keyboard, they can have a job *using* a keyboard.

MAN: Shut up. Everyone knows disabled people can't tweet.

CAROL: We're not all the same. *(a beat)* I'm – I'm not like that. I'm a *good* disabled -

NADINE: You can't be disabled and tweet. You can't be disabled and have friends. You can't be disabled and socialise or hold down a job or be valued, by society or by anyone.

DINO: Hector talked back to Achilles, to power. "My doom has come upon me; let me not then die ingloriously and without struggle. *Please*. Let me first do some great thing – to be told among men hereafter."

CAROL pauses.

MAN: I'd rather die than be disabled.

WOMAN: *(laughing)* God, same!

DINO: Then no god acts, intervenes. Keep an eye down here, but up there, yes? So wolf-gut Achilles was unstopped. Tongue cut, mute, skin crisp by unceasing sun, heels slit – metal kebab-sticked through, flesh torn by dragging horses, legs broken, ligaments lashed, pissed on and dirt eyed. Hector forever dead and mutilated – made defective, unbeautiful - in the golden glens of Elysium.

WOMAN: Fancy chairs, extra parking spaces, adapted homes.

MAN: We're footing the bill for their luxuaries.

WOMAN: Liquid diets, stoma bags, spare canes.

MAN: Buy them with your own money, shitstains Anyway, a prosthetic leg is just as good as a real one. We have adaptations now.

WOMAN: - and yoga,

MAN: so you're not really disabled, are you.

WOMAN: So shut up, stop trying to act special.

MAN: Stop wasting our money -

WOMAN: Our space

MAN: Our air

CAROL exits. Others shout in her direction.

MAN: Faker.

WOMAN: Parasite.

MAN: Fraud.

ALL: SCROUNGER

Act 2, Scene 2.

A desk with a chair behind it. A chair to the side of the desk. ABBY stands, holding the door open as JUNE enters the room. She is in her fifties, with warm rosy cheeks. JUNE sways when they walk, and stumbles into the chair. ABBY takes a seat.

ABBY: Good journey?

JUNE: Yes, I – the taxi got me here plenty early so I wouldn't be late.

ABBY: That's good. We all try our best to run on time, don't we Mrs-?

JUNE: June Pierce, Miss-?

ABBY: Abby. I'm trained as a

White noise plays – censoring ABBY.

ABBY: But now I'm carrying out these assessments.

JUNE: Oh, I did that too, before my mental health and leg kicked up a fuss. I took a leave

	from work and just haven't been up to going back.
ABBY:	Which is what we'll be discussing today. There's some paperwork I've got to fill in but I'll try to make it easy for you.
JUNE:	Thank you. I've been so worried -
ABBY:	Um, first, just – can I clarify if you arranged that taxi you got and therefore if you're able to plan the unfamiliar route you took to this assessment centre today?
JUNE:	Uh, yes, but I don't like phone calls -
ABBY:	*(as she writes)* No one does.
JUNE:	No, you don't understand. I get all, anxious and wound up and I get panic attacks sometimes from small, stupid, silly things.
ABBY:	Ok.
JUNE:	I don't have family. So the most I talk to people are the carers I pay to help me go

                    through my post, or cook for me when it hurts too bad to stand. So the call was tough, and talking now is tough but I've got to, don't I? Else -

ABBY: What is your diagnosis, June?

JUNE: I'm getting seen for anxiety, and my leg is /

ABBY: Seen? As in therapy? CBT?

JUNE: Yes, at first through a charity for six weeks then with a pri-private therapist.

ABBY: How long?

JUNE: It's been *(a pause)* seven or eight months.

ABBY: Any success?

JUNE: Ah, not yet.

ABBY: You can't always tell from the inside, can you?

JUNE: No, but I *think* it's helping.

ABBY: Do you think you'll be *(beat)* better within the year?

JUNE: I don't know. I've been struggling for so long and I don't, I don't know yet -

ABBY: Ok, that's ok. We can skip that question.

JUNE: That was a question? On your form?

ABBY: Yes, with diagnoses I ask what it is, how it affects you, and when you might recover.

JUNE: Oh. I see.

ABBY: Can we talk about your leg?

JUNE: Yes, of course. It's always popped out of its socket, since I was a kid and that. But one day, like four years back, it shifted and now it's in constant pain. I take medication for it but I, I can't walk right. I collapse sometimes. *You* know the job, I can't be sitting for a shift – I have to walk to and fro, and I'd switch to office work but my anxiety is on the up. I couldn't hack that. I'd never make it in, I'd. Retraining is tough and I, my hands hurt, I can't hold pens always and I feel so, so -

The claimant begins to breathe heavily, an oncoming panic attack. ABBY rushes forwards to help, with a soothing voice.

ABBY: June, June it's ok. I will make sure to write that down, for you. June, may I hold your hand for you? *(a pause)* June, I'm going to hold your hand for a moment. Breathe with me.

JUNE: I'm sorry. I'm sorry. I should be getting better. I want to be getting better. I'm sorry.

ABBY: I know. I know, June. Don't worry, hun.

JUNE: I'm sorry.

ABBY: Don't worry. Or at least, you don't need to apologise.

JUNE: *(pause)* Thank you. *(deep breath)* Where, where were we up to?

ABBY: Are you sure you want to continue?

JUNE: I don't feel like I have a choice.

ABBY: Ok, June. How far can you walk? Is it more than twenty metres?

JUNE: I, uh. If – if there was a fire or emergency, I *think* I could.

ABBY: Let me clarify, June. Can you walk more than twenty metres *without* pain? Can you do it reliably, every day even, without any doubt or consequential relapse of other symptoms? And would it take you no longer than twice the amount of time than a, a normal person?

JUNE: No. No, definitely not. Some days I can't walk at all, but on my best days I can slowly stagger about. I don't really walk anymore. It's too draining and it brings on

	bad days. I get my food delivered. I'm so, it's like I'm ice, Abby. Isolated and – and scared, Abby. I'm frozen, so cold, I can't – Abby.
ABBY:	I'm sorry to hear that, June.
JUNE:	*(her tone changes)* It's not all doom and gloom though. I have friends visit, sometimes. And I'm thinking I might try to earn a few bob online, website design and such. Long distance tutoring, maybe. I do *want* to work, I just don't know how yet – I don't think I could do something physical, is all. I just – I'm not a right fit for most things anymore.
ABBY:	I gotcha, I know. I'm going to write down the answers you've told me and add in some more to build your case.

JUNE: Thank you. Thank you so much. You've been so kind. Nothing like I was worried about. I heard stories.

ABBY: If, for some strange reason, they put you in the standard or work related activity group you'll receive a lower rate of payment, but it should be noted down that your disability *does* limit you.

JUNE: I thought you were the one deciding?

ABBY: No, I write about this meeting and that accompanies the evidence you sent in and another person looks at both to decide.

JUNE: Ok. Thank you for explaining that, and-and. Thank you for just being nice.

ABBY: It's no problem. It's the absolute minimum to expect, ok? *(a beat, ABBY returns to the form)* Is there anything else you want to tell me to support your claim?

JUNE: No, No I. Everything is in with the evidence and letters I sent. All the proof. I don't know why I even got asked to come, because apparently that's not mandatory so I was worried. It's not like you can just, glance or chitchat and know what someone lives with. There's a lot of shame with *(pause)* well, any struggle, I suppose. Disability. I don't want to be disabled, and I often don't think I am. I just, I call myself "*ill*" because then I can face the day, Abby. Anything but disabled, you know? People'd rather be dead than disabled. And I don't know how to live if I think like that. Like I used to, before I had - struggles.

ABBY: I'm sorry to ask, June, but do you sometimes think that? Want to be dead?

JUNE: I don't want to be how I am right now. Sometimes that makes me less cautious.

ABBY: Is that, do you think that way often?

JUNE: On and off. Therapy helps.

ABBY: I'm glad it helps you.

JUNE: Today, so am I.

JUNE exits. ABBY fills in her form. For a time there is peace. Then ABBY's EMPLOYER storms in.

EMPLOYER: What do you think that was?

ABBY: I think - ?

EMPLOYER: You do know I was monitoring that, yes?

ABBY: Yes, of course. What did I do wrong?

EMPLOYER: *(with a disbelieving laugh)* I have a list. I didn't catch *everything* you did, who knows if I could have with the frequency, since you started going *so* wrong *so* early in that assessment. You may well be terminated early at this rate.

ABBY: Please, talk me through it. I don't think I *(beat)* comprehend -

EMPLOYER: No, I really don't think you do. First, what was with the chitchat, the rapport? You're not here to make friends with the claimant. By all means, get the truth from 'em, but don't let their little details cloud your judgement.

ABBY: Is this about time keeping, again? Is there no time for please and thank you in this role?

EMPLOYER: Next, you actually explained without being required to. Unbelievable.

ABBY: Why? And why is that a problem?

EMPLOYER: If the claimant is confused they will ask for clarification, which shows that they are more than capable of clear communication and therefore can be recommended as not disabled, fit for a role in the service industries. Or, they understood without questioning you – which makes them ideal for any industry.

ABBY: If they don't understand the question they might not give an accurate answer. That would be detrimental to the whole assessment. It would be inaccurate.

EMPLOYER: *(flatly)* Inaccurate.

ABBY: Yes. Some disabilities surely mean that *(beat)* some people can't work – or at least need the support PIP offers them in addition to working. So I'll report that, when I see it.

EMPLOYER: When you see it? Abby, your job isn't to help people. Your role is to ask questions, fill in that form, and try to see through all the nonsense they present and *(pause)* report optimistically. Everyone is simply more capable then they think they are.

ABBY: Is that how it is?

The EMPLOYER picks up ABBY's paperwork, and tuts.

EMPLOYER: Now we need to fix this report of yours, before filing it.

ABBY: What?

EMPLOYER: Foremost, you can't write *that*. It's *inaccurate*.

ABBY: She had a panic attack!

EMPLOYER: She did not.

ABBY: She definitely did.

EMPLOYER: She was *wheezing*, it was only a light cough. And, moreover, she made eye contact, she was well-kempt with clean clothes. All signs of a clear, clean, healthy mental state.

ABBY: And what's not? How can you tell from the outside, a thirty minute – if that – meeting?

EMPLOYER: They'd be rocking back and forth if there were a problem.

ABBY: And would you have me put that down to their preference? How they like to sit? Maybe the chair's uncomfortable and they're adjusting!

EMPLOYER: Watch your tone, missy.

ABBY: It doesn't seem right.

EMPLOYER: You are a trainee here. You do not know right from wrong. Now, you held her hand. So you know her grip is fine. She can handle a pen, a knife for dinner, a box. She could stack shelves, at least, or sign slips at a bank. She's no problem cooking or eating — she's fat enough for that to be obvious - /

ABBY: You can't tell someone's diet from how they look.

EMPLOYER: You can.

ABBY: Some people are just shaped different, or their medication makes them swell or even – you do know that the body's first response to malnourishment is to store any food as fat. Looks are deceptive. It doesn't directly correlate.

EMPLOYER: True. Which is why you can't prove she *hasn't* made herself that way, through her own poor judgement. And since you didn't ask, we'll have to assume such conditions are reversible with support. That's what we say in the report.

ABBY: So will she get support, then? Keep the financial payments, the Motability car, whatever carers she has. All that hinges on this shallow assessment.

EMPLOYER: *(pause)* Abby, I know this is hard and you're not used to it. But it's not our job to *care*.

Act 2, Scene 3.

"Pain Management" is hung like bunting. SPEAKER is a fast talking, smooth talking white man. He allows no interruption. His audience is a dozen puppets flown in from above, dangling with visible string and clutching their mobility aids. He looms over them and may manipulate the puppets, never pausing due to their pained gasps or cries.

SPEAKER: Overcoming pain. Reclaim your life. Manage your time. Yes, to overcome your pain, you must first understand it and learn new ways of managing your discomfort. To tear yourself free from the bonds of pain, acknowledge that there is no pain. But live with it, accept that this is part of you, and do not let your disabilities define your limitations. Walk with a limp? You're just walking wrong. I'll teach you. Don't use a wall, a stick, don't use your chair. These "adaptations" hold you back. They let you get comfortable with the idea that you shouldn't strive anymore. That your life is at a certain standard. Lift yourselves up, better yourselves. You could do better. You would be happy if you tried. If you're not happy, and of course you're not, you've let disabilities disable you, then you haven't tried hard enough. Don't call yourself disabled, that's an excuse. You just want attention, you idiot. You don't *believe* in yourself.

At this point, the SPEAKER slaps a puppet on the back; it falls. He grabs another by the throat and shakes them.

SPEAKER: How many pain killers are you on? Five, ten? You shouldn't be on so many, it's a waste of resources. Even one is too many! *(He lets the puppet go)* Quit them all! I'll write to your GP, I'll tell them to stop the prescriptions, no more painkillers! I'll show you how to stop, how to find relief otherwise! Pain is often just in the brain, *(he prods one in the head)* or the synapses, but usually in the brain. And the brain can be distracted with mild, mild pleasure. While some self-medicate with the, with marijuana, which is just as bad as prescribed medication. Instead, find a cat and stroke it, pet a dog, have a hug with someone you love! And your pain is gone! We're just trying to help. We're helping. Don't you want to be better? You don't want to? Then don't complain, you'll overcome. You'll be fine, you'll be happy again. Don't you want to be happy? Be one of us. Obey me. No one is really disabled, you've just thought yourself ill. Think different thoughts! Be healthy again! Anyone can do it! So why haven't you?

The SPEAKER points at the audience.

SPEAKER: Stop flinching. Stop sighing. Stop holding your wounds, your achey bits. Stop leaning, stop sitting, stop complaining. Shut up. Take up less room. Be small. Be silent. Be stupid with pain. It's not real. Tell yourself it's not real. Tell us it's not real. Admit that you've been lying. Wasting resources. And remember to fill in this form. Rate me ten out of ten, or I'll have words with you.

Lights go down.

Act 2, Scene 4.

The sound of smashing glass. Light changes to reveal the living room, as before. HANNAH is carefully clearing shattered glass from the floor. CAROL stands aside.

CAROL: I should've told you.

HANNAH: You should've told me.

CAROL: I should have.

HANNAH: And you didn't.

CAROL: You don't need to worry /

HANNAH: I am worried.

CAROL: Well, don't. It's done now.

HANNAH: Nearly done.

CAROL: You're right.

HANNAH: *(a pause)* So, when is it? When do we have to go?

CAROL: You don't have to come with /

HANNAH: Of course I am coming / with you

CAROL: You have work.

HANNAH: Work, smerk. I can call in sick.

CAROL: Again? Hannah, no. Your boss - /

HANNAH: Can fire me. I'll get another job. Easily.

CAROL: But will it-? Hannah, all this job hopping, never progressing. You had potential, you still could do something. Make something of yourself.

HANNAH has done away with the shards. She holds CAROLs hands in hers.

HANNAH: I can and one day I will, mum. This is temporary. And what are you doing distracting / me?

CAROL: It's not a distraction, it's necessary. This – you – are important. Just as important.

HANNAH: Sure, but what we're *currently* discussing is *you* and this face to face assessment thingy.

CAROL: Hannah, it will be fine. You said it yourself, they just want to check we're not – I'm not – lying. They… they will see that. Scaremonger. Propaganda, lies, fear – none of that is real, none of that can be real. I'll be fine. And you – you'll be better than fine, Hannah.

HANNAH: I am /

CAROL: No. I want you to have more, chase what you want. You're still young, you have a body – you have strength and a heart and so, so much more than me.

HANNAH: Mum.

CAROL: Don't waste it. Don't throw it aside, not because of me.

HANNAH: I'm not throwing anything away. I'm holding onto you. I'm helping you.

CAROL: Not enough! *(silence)*

HANNAH: *(direct address)* I say nothing.

CAROL: Not – Hannah, I don't. I don't mean. Just, I just – sometimes you're not where you should be or I call out and you don't – aren't. I can't have you all to myself, and I – I – you aren't able to *(beat)*. I'm – I don't want to be a burden / on you.

HANNAH: You're not, mum.

CAROL: I am, Hannah.

HANNAH: I love you.

CAROL: And I love you more, more than you could love me – since I first held you, since I first felt you, kicking inside me. And nothing, Hannah, nothing – *(beat)* I want you to be happy.

HANNAH: I'm happy.

CAROL: Happier.

HANNAH: I am /

CAROL: Happier than me.

HANNAH: *(direct address)* I say nothing.

CAROL: *(direct address)* I say nothing.

CAROL and HANNAH turn out to face the audience.

CAROL: *(direct address)* I make her promise me something.

HANNAH: Ok.

CAROL: *(direct address)* She'll go back to her studies. She'll get a nice job. She *will* surpass me.

HANNAH: *(direct address)* We go, together, to the assessment centre. Google tells us that it is not disability friendly. Stairs to every door, no hand rails. Thoughtless, really, how architecture itself can speak: says "no, you are not welcome. No, you may not pass. No, no, no."

Act 2, Scene 5.

The door is closed. ABBY sits at her desk and waits for her next appointment to begin. The door handle wriggles and rattles before the JOSH enters. The door looks heavy. The claimant, a twenty-something black man, walks without any limp and takes a seat.

ABBY: Hello, Mr?

JOSH: Josh Sandhu. I hope I'm in the right room.

ABBY: Yes, you are. Now, if you're ready I have a few questions to ask.

JOSH: Ask away.

ABBY: Firstly, please remind me what your condition is?

JOSH: Did you not read what I sent?

ABBY: Sometimes that paperwork doesn't get to the assessment centre in time, but thankfully I'm here to report on what I see

> in this room and your evidence will of course be used in the final consideration.

JOSH: That sounded very rehearsed.

ABBY: *(with a laugh)* It was, a little bit.

JOSH: I do cold calling for a living, so I can recognise the tone.

ABBY: So you work?

JOSH: Yes, full time. But I just got diagnosed, see. Cancer.

ABBY: Oh god.

JOSH: Yeah, that's what I thought.

ABBY: Do you know – do you know any more, yet?

JOSH: Brain. Inoperable. But I'm still working, for as long as I'm able. I get dizzy spells and memory issues and migraines like nothing else. Told the GP too late, waiting times, too – you know?

ABBY: I hate to ask, but is it terminal? Which, I have to clarify, this form means you'd have less than six months.

JOSH: I told them I don't want to know. Me wife knows, so she can contact the hospice if I get that bad, and the kids know *something* is up.

ABBY: That must be so, so hard for you. *(a beat)* So let's see about this form. If you qualify for the Personal Independence Payment and what we can calculate your score will be as your condition presumably deteriorates. I'm sorry that this is the way the process goes, Josh. I really am.

JOSH: I've heard that cancer patients wouldn't be called in for this face to face appointment. But lo-and-behold, you know?

ABBY: I don't know how they pick who to send. Sometimes it seems like they just send everyone, every year or year and a half.

Sorry, I only know what I know. *(a beat)* Ok, Josh. Some of these questions will seem a little irrelevant but we've got to get through them. First, can you safely and reliably plan, cook, and eat your food?

JOSH: Yes.

ABBY: Good. Can you plan and make a journey along an unfamiliar route, like you did today to get this place?

JOSH: Yes. I drive, so.

ABBY: Can you wash, without prompting?

JOSH: Of – yes. Yes I can. I wipe and everything.

ABBY: Do you watch TV?

JOSH: *(with a laugh)* Yes? How is that relevant? Um, yes, I do.

ABBY: Got a favourite?

JOSH: Now that's definitely not on the form, is it?

ABBY: No, but we got time for it. I like The Great Gatsby, myself.

JOSH: Ah, the crumbling American Dream, eh? Are you a fan of watching, I don't know, modest try-hards against the *(beat)* backdrop of corruption and crumbing, beautiful illusions?

ABBY: I like the actors.

JOSH: Ah, Leonardo DiCaprio.

ABBY: Tobey Maguire.

JOSH: No!

ABBY: Yes. Now, I told you mine.

JOSH: Oh, now I'm cornered.

ABBY: Yup.

JOSH: Ok, don't tell anyone this, *(sucks in a breath between his teeth)* but I really liked the Spongebob movie.

ABBY: Wow. The one with Hasselhoff.

JOSH: Yes. I've been busy with work, I haven't really seen anything since. Not whole films, all the way through. I fall asleep really early on. It's one of the only films I remember in full.

ABBY: Nice.

The pair smile. Abruptly, ABBY recalls that she has an assessment to complete.

ABBY: Anyway, getting on. Are you on any medication and are there side effects?

JOSH: Yes and yes. I've brought in my prescription, I can't spell or pronounce half the stuff. And, I've only noticed *(quietly)* constipation *(normally)* and the rest I just assume is the… the.

JOSH gestures to his head. ABBY nods.

ABBY: Thanks.

There is a knock at the door. ABBY and JOSH look to the door. Another knock. ABBY goes to the door. Behind it stands EMPLOYER.

EMPLOYER: May I speak with you for a moment, Abby?

ABBY: Of course. Excuse me, Josh.

JOSH: I can wait.

ABBY and EMPLOYER exit to a different room. The claimant cannot hear any of this and fiddles with his sleeves, checks his phone. We see both inside the assessment room and the corridor simultaneously.

ABBY: Is there something wrong?

EMPLOYER: A few things. Thankfully less than last time.

ABBY: Ok. *(a deep breath in)* Hit me with it.

EMPLOYER: I know you struggle to *(beat)* cut out all the chatter and *friendliness*. But you really have to. No smiling, Abby. No jokes. Read from the script, do not stray from it unless they specifically ask for clarification. You do not make this easier for them. That's not fair to others who must answer every question solemnly, reporting one condition after another.

ABBY: *(nodding)* Ok. No smiling. Read the script. Got it.

There is a pause.

EMPLOYER: Abby. *(sighs)* I don't think you fully appreciate what your record shows, so far. Abby, look. You're badly off target.

The EMPLOYER shows ABBY the clipboard.

ABBY: Am I? I mean, I thought 20% rejection recommendations was kind of high, but I'm hovering over that.

EMPLOYER: Twenty percent reje-. I see the problem. Right. Abby, you've misread the sheet. Our quota is to *reject* eighty percent of applications. Only one in five is supposed

	to leave this building with a recommendation for receiving PIP.
ABBY:	How? *(pause)* Honestly, how? Everyone I've seen is disabled. There's no fraudsters. There's no one who isn't struggling.
EMPLOYER:	And that's the conundrum, Abby. That's the impossible situation we're in. We have to obey the quota or the lot of us can be replaced. *(pauses)* Abby, you said it yourself. *We have bills to pay.*
ABBY:	*(with quiet dread)* Bills. My flat, the loans.
EMPLOYER:	It's just a job.
ABBY:	*(a beat)* That man in there, and the woman earlier today. This is more than a job to them, it's financial security. Peace of mind. The difference between food and a home and nothing.

EMPLOYER: And isn't our job that to you? Financial security, peace of mind. It's what your *wages* get you. Look, Abby, I know it's tough but if they're desperate they'll just apply again or they'll make it to tribunal – where an independent panel will just overturn any of the nonsense we have to write. The right people will get the support they need, backdated too. We're not harming anyone, just *(beat)* inconveniencing them.

ABBY: And I need to start inconveniencing people?

EMPLOYER: To keep your job? Yes. *(Pause)* I hate to be blunt, but to hit target at this stage? So I can end your probation and stop breathing down your neck? You need to deny every single person who walks through that door, regardless of their condition. I've done the figures, B, and you

>   can scrape by this month if you just. *(beat)*
>   Stop smiling. Stop befriending them. Write
>   your report and move onto the next
>   person.

The door opens. ABBY walks back into the room. JOSH jolts to look.

JOSH: That was a while. Everything ok?

ABBY: Yes.

JOSH: Oh, good.

There is a silence.

JOSH: Are you sure you're ok?

ABBY: I think it's best we continue the assessment.

JOSH: Right you are.

ABBY: No symptoms, was it?

JOSH: Ah, no – I do have /

ABBY: And it's not terminal.

JOSH: That I know.

ABBY: Otherwise you are a fully functioning human being, with a job on top.

JOSH: *(beat)* I suppose, but I wouldn't say /

ABBY: I believe that concludes this face to face assessment. You will receive a letter in the post with the final decision. Goodbye.

Lights down.

Act 2, Scene 6.

CAROL and HANNAH enter through the door to the assessment office, speaking with each other. CAROL walks with her stick and HANNAH holds her other arm. DINO speaks to the audience.

DINO: *(direct address)* Sleep,

CAROL: I didn't sleep.

DINO: *(direct address)* Before whom all things bow, did not have a hold of you.

HANNAH: We'll sleep in tomorrow.

DINO: *(direct address)* You sleep and have forgotten me; you / loved me

HANNAH: Love you, mum.

DINO: *(direct address)* Living, but now that I am dead you think of –

HANNAH: Abby?

DINO: *(direct address)* - me no further.

HANNAH: B? *(a significant pause)* oh.

ABBY: I'm, I assess PIP claimants now. Or at least, I run the face to face interviews. It's the/

HANNAH: That interview you went for.

ABBY: Yeah.

HANNAH: The job you –

ABBY: Yes.

HANNAH: That's what we're here for. We just, we've told the front desk that we're here on time.

ABBY: Are you the 12 o'clock?

HANNAH: Yes.

ABBY: If I'm – If I'm your, I have to be a professional. Impartial.

HANNAH: Of course, B.

ABBY: I'm still on probation.

HANNAH: Ok.

ABBY: I can't lose this job. I, I'll lose the flat, default on the. Hannah. Don't hate me. I'm just, I'm following the script.

ABBY becomes the ASSESSOR. HANNAH is seated a little behind CAROL. CAROL is trembling.

ASSESSOR: Can you plan, prepare, and safely cook a three course meal?

CAROL: No.

ASSESSOR: Can you use the microwave?

CAROL: *(a pause)* Yes.

ASSESSOR: Then yes. Do you require prompting to eat and look after yourself?

CAROL: Yes. If-if I'm not encouraged I won't.

ASSESSOR: Won't what?

CAROL: Eat, wash, rest. I don't – I can't look after myself.

ASSESSOR: Have you tried setting alarms? Scheduling yourself?

CAROL: I don't, I just. I've tried.

ASSESSOR: Hm. And what medications are you on? *(HANNAH goes to speak)* Don't you answer, I want to hear it from you.

CAROL: We-we brought a, all my medication is in this bag. One box of each, to show you.

ASSESSOR: Why would you do that? We don't need that.

CAROL: We thought, we were told -

ASSESSOR: You've misunderstood then. Give me a list.

HANNAH: *(pause)* It says it all – we wrote it already in the form.

ASSESSOR: And I need a list. *(a beat)* You have a prescription with you?

CAROL: Yes. I meant to hand it in, have another lot prep-

ASSESSOR: Give it to me.

The CARER does so.

CAROL: Will I get it back?

ASSESSOR: No. Now, tell me more about you. What do you watch on TV?

CAROL: I, the news, sometimes.

ASSESSOR: Do you have pets?

CAROL: I had a dog. He died.

ASSESSOR: When did you have a dog?

CAROL: We, I got him before I, before the op. When I was normal.

ASSESSOR: And how'd you get here today? You drove? Bus?

CAROL: *(a pause)* A, a taxi. I can't. I only drive short distances.

HANNAH: Well known, preplanned.

ASSESSOR: But you can drive further?

HANNAH: No, they can't. I accompany –

ASSESSOR: If you planned. If you had a map. If you googled it first, you can do it?

HANNAH: Abby.

ASSESSOR: It is Ms. Thomson, right now.

HANNAH: *(a pause)* Ms. *(a pause)* Ms Thomson. I must accompany my mother. You know – we've said this.

ASSESSOR: And you work?

HANNAH: A few hours a week.

ASSESSOR: So you leave her unattended.

HANNAH: Only on days that she'll be well enough.

ASSESSOR: She's well enough for-?

HANNAH: When she can. When she doesn't need to get to and from rooms, when she can sleep through the shift instead. If she

                    wants or needs anything, she needs
                    someone.

ASSESSOR: Is this the case?

CAROL: Yes.

ASSESSOR: You're powerless without support.

CAROL: In a, yes.

ASSESSOR: Though you look well.

CAROL: Do I?

ASSESSOR: Are you suicidal? Answer the question. This is a question I have to ask. Are you suicidal, Carol?

CAROL: *(a pause)* yes.

ASSESSOR: How often are you suicidal?

CAROL: *(a pause)* Every day

ASSESSOR: Have you tried?

CAROL: *(a pause)* Yes.

HANNAH: *(quietly)* I never knew that.

ASSESSOR: If you're really in that much pain why haven't you succeeded?

CAROL: *(a pause)* My family. They'd miss me. They said -

ASSESSOR: Why did you fail to kill yourself, Carol?

CAROL: *(a pause)* I don't know. I was found *(a pause)* in time.

ASSESSOR: Can you use the bath?

CAROL: *(a pause)* No.

ASSESSOR: The shower?

CAROL: *(a pause)* No.

ASSESSOR: How do you wash?

CAROL: *(a pause)* With a, a cloth. And I can't reach. I get help.

ASSESSOR: Every day?

CAROL: *(a pause)* No, no I only. I only wash when I'm well enough to –

ASSESSOR: No, do you need that help every day? Are you ever *well*?

CAROL: *(a pause)* No.

ASSESSOR: You're saying you're never well?

CAROL: No.

ASSESSOR: Why not?

CAROL: *(a pause)* I. I don't know. My doctor says –

ASSESSOR: What about using the toilet?

CAROL: *(a pause)* I have, I have adaptations around the house. But I can't, I struggle to sit down, I have to throw myself onto – and sometimes I don't. I fall. And I can't get up.

ASSESSOR: And when you don't fall? You are fine.

CAROL: No. I can't get up either, off the loo. I need help. I call and get lifted off, most times.

>   And when, when I'm out, I-I have
>   accidents. I don't, I usually don't make it.

ASSESSOR: And then -

CAROL: I get embarrassed and humiliated and I feel so fucking stupid and I have to go home and try to clean myself.

ASSESSOR: So you *can* clean yourself?

CAROL: I try. I.

ASSESSOR: I need to go back and edit that response then.

CAROL: Why?

ASSESSOR: You can bathe just fine. *(a pause)* And you dress yourself?

CAROL: I get help.

ASSESSOR: Do you *need* any help dressing? *(a beat)* and what about reading? Do you *need* help with that?

CAROL: *(a pause)* No. *(a pause)* I have glasses?

ASSESSOR: And socialising? You go out, yes?

CAROL: No.

ASSESSOR: No?

CAROL: I get anxious

ASSESSOR: But you have friends who visit,

CAROL: No *(a pause)* I'm too. I don't like them seeing how I live.

ASSESSOR: But you talk just fine.

Silence

ASSESSOR: How far can you walk unaided?

CAROL: *(a pause)* I don't know. Not far.

ASSESSOR: Shall we see?

CAROL: I. I don't.

ASSESSOR: So you're refusing? You can refuse but I have to say you refused.

CAROL: *(a pause)* Ok.

ASSESSOR: *(abrupt, rude)* Get up *(a long pause, then nicely)* in your own time, when you're ready.

CAROL puts her hands on the arm rest. She leans forwards. Slowly she pushes up. She cannot hold it. She rests again and breathes. She takes a deep breath and tries again. She pushes herself upright and slightly forward, using the table to then lean on. She is in pain, but does not sound out. She holds onto her pride. She is trembling. She sniffs, holding herself together. She pushes upright and leans away from the table. She has not yet taken a single step. She shuffles her feet forward, sliding one across the ground. She sways, HANNAH half-catches CAROL, holding her upright.

ASSESSOR: Without aid. It's important. It's what the question asks. We must complete the form together. The government must have its answers.

HANNAH lets go. CAROL takes another step forward. And another. She has moved all of four feet. CAROL shakes her head. HANNAH moves the chair so it is under CAROL, then physically supports CAROL, holding her back and arm to lower her, to sit CAROL down. The ASSESSOR tuts.

ASSESSOR: And when will you be well?

CAROL: I, I don't know. Maybe never? The doctors don't help much. They see me and send me away. I have medication but I'm not getting better, it's only to manage the symptoms then to control the side effects and –

ASSESSOR: Will you be better in six months?

CAROL: No, no I –

ASSESSOR: Will you be fixed in a year? I have to write this down.

CAROL: I don't think so –

ASSESSOR: So you refused to answer the question.

HANNAH: She won't be well. Ever, ever again.

ASSESSOR: I see.

HANNAH: What's *(a pause)* What's going to happen next? What's the process?

ASSESSOR: I'll type up my report; what I've seen, what you've answered. That and the form you submitted will be processed together by a different member of staff, who will look at the two documents together and compile a third. Then a different member of staff will review the documents and decide what your score will be. There are two categories that are considered: the daily living component and the mobility. You'll need to score at least 8 in both parts to get Standard rate PIP, and over 12 in each for Enhanced. And *(a long pause, then fast)* I shouldn't be telling you this, because we're not actively allowed to help, but if you – if

>   you disagree with the final decision, please
>   complete a Mandatory Reconsideration
>   application straight away. You have near
>   no time to launch one, else the entire claim
>   is invalid.

There is a knock at the door.

CAROL: Abby, please -

ASSESSOR: I can't help you. Please. See your own way out.

HANNAH: Are you really going to do this?

CAROL: Hannah.

HANNAH: Just, treat us like this? And expect us to /

ASSESSOR: / See your own way out.

HANNAH: Abby.

ASSESSOR: I can't help you.

HANNAH: *(pause)* I can't believe you. This, this job – your commission – over us /

CAROL: *(frightful)* Hannah don't say anything. Don't, please don't jeopardise / this.

ASSESSOR: You think I don't know what – This is my job. We don't help.

The door opens. A call from off stage.

OFF: You have another appointment in five!

ASSESSOR: *(beat, then recalling)* There's always a price, Abby Thomson.

HANNAH: There's always a price, Hannah Joyce.

CLAIMANT: There's always - /

Act 2, Scene 7.

We can hear a train approaching. It gets closer and louder.

CAROL: *(direct address)* I was going to complain about the stress, worry, anxiety and depression it causes me. Being judged by someone who doesn't know me or my health problems both physical and mental health. Then the long in-person assessments. Then the wait for a decision, and reports not being accurate and the assessment ignoring what I wrote and what my doctor wrote. It's *damaging*. It takes months and months to recover, it makes my health *worse,* just to get another type of assessment, my ESA, just a few months later. I'm in the support group, I can't work, why am I being forced to be reassessed and reassessed again? I've never going to get better. I'm never going to get back what I've lost. This is my life. This just, it puts me through unnecessary worry, depression. But I won't, can't write anything to them, I can't make a complaint - I'm afraid it will be used as evidence that I *can* communicate. They'll say I can work. That I don't need any support, that I don't struggle, that I'm not ill. They can use anything against me. I heard that they spy on us, now, with drones. I won't open the curtains.

HANNAH: *(direct address)* Even if we go through the reconsideration form or tribunal, it's no excuse to do that to us. To my mum. She - No, I'm not gonna say it. What kind of country does this?

DINO: *(direct address)* It can't be done, lass. You can't make them care. They hate us, they utterly hate us. There's no way to be a good enough disabled, a good enough disabled who is real and genuine and not a cheat – and be alive, and need welfare. They don't see that. Either you're not disabled enough to get support, or else you need it – right – and here's the thing. If you need help because you're honestly disabled, then why are you still alive? Why didn't you die? Just kill yourself already. You'll never amount to anything, you are nothing, you're a burden, you're a cost, an expense, a waste, an administrative fee, a stain. Nought but dust to the stars themselves. Woosh. Let it end. They say they care, that they're so kind. But they show us this, what's true.

HANNAH: *(direct address)* Pay attention.

CAROL: *(direct address)* We are nothing to them. We are nothing.

DINO: *(direct address)* I study the universe.

HANNAH: *(direct address)* Shit. I didn't make you a tea.

ABBY: *(direct address)* I had the distinct feeling I was talking to a god.

DINO: *(direct address)* You must think I'm mad.

ABBY: *(direct address)* It's not my job to care.

HANNAH: *(direct address)* I love you mum.

ABBY: *(direct address)* Plato's Prime Mover, I thought.

CAROL: *(direct address)* I had a dog. He died. A cat visits, though.

HANNAH: *(direct address)* Shrivelled up like a dead leaf. A shadow of a bird passing by.

ABBY: *(direct address)* I caused everything – I moved the first thing, but now have nothing to do with you.

CAROL: *(direct address)* This shouldn't be so bloody difficult.

ABBY: *(direct address)* I can't help you. Please.

HANNAH: *(direct address)* Are you really going to do this?

ABBY: *(direct address)* See your own way out.

DINO: *(direct address)* You're afraid.

Train sounds out, so loud, light implying its path. The light cuts out with a scream. Silence.

CAROL: *(direct address)* What's going to happen next?

Black out.

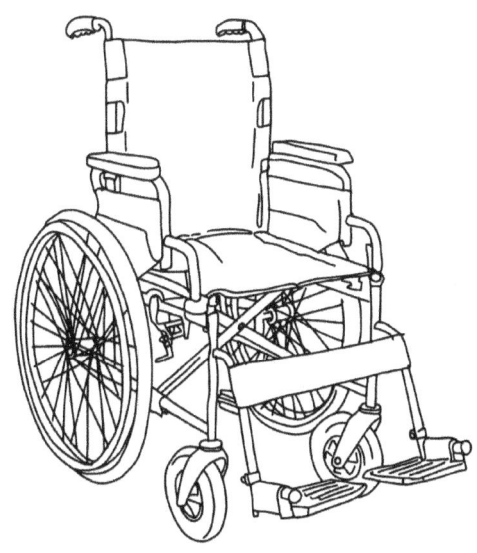

www.ingramcontent.com/pod-product-compliance
Lightning Source LLC
LaVergne TN
LVHW051219070526
838200LV00064B/4965